*Connell Guide
to
Samuel Beckett's*

Waiting for Godot

*by
Sophie Ratcliffe*

Contents

Beginnings	1
What happens in *Waiting for Godot*?	4
Did Beckett intend the play to fail?	5
How funny is *Waiting for Godot*?	8
Humans or animals?	12
Who is Godot?	14
Why are Beckett's stage directions so precise?	16
What is Beckett telling us about life?	19
Why is repetition so important in the play?	24
Does Beckett mock the idea of human solidarity?	27
Five facts about Beckett and *Waiting for Godot*	28
What should we make of the "climax"?	32
Does *Waiting for Godot* belong to the 'Theatre of the Absurd'?	35
Further Reading	41

Beginnings

In a small Parisian apartment in the winter of 1948, a little-known Irish novelist was suffering from writer's block. Having reached what he felt was an "impasse" with his prose works, he opened a notebook and began something new. After four months, he reached the final line. The result was *En Attendant Godot*, a play for a cast of five, which he later translated into the two act tragi-comedy, *Waiting for Godot*. Beckett himself once joked that the play was "a mess". The public felt differently, and the impact of this drama, which shattered conventional expectations of form and meaning, is still being felt today. As Mary Bryden notes, "despite his non-appearance", the character of Godot has proved an enduringly popular fictional touchstone – a kind of "pop culture ghost" who "materialises" in the most unexpected places, from cartoons to adverts for car insurance. The play itself has a darker history. While praised for its control and linguistic beauty, readers and critics agree that like much of Beckett's work, it is difficult. Interpreting the text can be confusing, and inconclusive. As a vision of life it seems, at first, to be both depressing and harsh.

Some critics have dwelt on its complex textual history. While *En Attendant Godot* was published in 1952, American audiences had to wait two years for their Godot – translated by Beckett himself –

while a version only reached British bookshelves in 1965. Although Beckett's mother-tongue was English, he often chose to write in French. He then put himself through what he termed the "wastes and wilds of self-translation". The existence of two different, but equally valid, versions of the same work creates multiple difficulties for readers. Others have been perplexed by the plot of the play itself. Is this tale of two men waiting for an appointment with a mysterious Mr Godot meant to symbolise something – a parable, or metaphor perhaps, for the condition of mankind? Does the road they wait on stand for the journey of life?

Not so long ago, before the first production, Beckett and his romantic partner Suzanne spent their own lives on the road, as they escaped from the Gestapo. They were forced from Paris and went to Vichy, France. Knowing this biographical background, one can pick up on elements within the play which reflect an atmosphere of the world at war. Characters endure long waits, crossed wires and low resources. Strange, tyrannous figures appear. There is even a brief mention of Vaucluse, the region in which Beckett and Suzanne waited for the liberation of Nazi-occupied France. However, a simplistic biographical reading of the play is near impossible, as well as unrewarding. Beckett carefully preserved the anonymity of his tramps (or clowns, as they first appeared). Their provenance is never made clear and the play purposely takes place in an indefinite location.

Indeed, the fact that Beckett does not, in this, or any work, appear directly to address historical and political concerns led critics such as György Lukaçs to feel that his work is escapist. Beckett's purported failure to use the theatre as a tool for social change – together with the agonising positions that he puts his characters in, as well as his actors – has attracted the charge that his theatre is uninteresting, or even inhumane.

Such accusations certainly bear no relation to Beckett's life. Born on Good Friday, 13 April 1906, he was a brilliant student destined for a great academic career. However, after spending a year teaching in Paris, he rejected the secure life of academia for a precarious existence reviewing, writing and travelling in Europe. He eventually settled in Paris – and, when the Germans invaded, Beckett began to work for the French Resistance, narrowly escaping capture. His quiet heroism during the war led to him being awarded the Croix de Guerre in 1945, and he went on to work for the Irish Red Cross in Normandy.

A careful viewing, or reading, of *Waiting for Godot* reveals Beckett's sense for the devastations of his time that he had witnessed, which he referred to as a vision of "humanity in ruins", and an exploration of what a human drama might have to offer. It is, as critic William Saroyan writes, "an important play, perhaps one of the most important of all times".

What happens in *Waiting for Godot*?

The plot itself seems designed to disappoint the audience. Two men sit under a tree on a country road, waiting for a meeting with a Mr Godot. Their names are Estragon and Vladimir, though they refer to each other by the diminutives Gogo and Didi. At the end of both the first and the second act, a small boy arrives to let them know that Mr Godot will not come. Though they are interrupted by a man named Pozzo, who is accompanied by his servant, Lucky, nothing of great significance appears to happen. At the end of each act they decide to leave, but do not move from the stage

The play, which is a struggle to understand, begins with its own small struggle. As the curtain opens on a near-empty stage, we watch a man attempting to remove his boot with little success, pulling at it, panting, failing, resting, resuming, only to try again. But the failure is not his alone. As the man, Estragon, speaks, the audience, too, are placed in difficulties. Who is he? Where is he? When he speaks the play's opening line – "Nothing to be done" – is he referring to the state of his footwear, or is he making a more general comment on life? Vladimir's entrance promises some clarity at first, as he addresses his companion with an air of familiarity – "so there you are again". However, Estragon's bewildered and cynical response – "Am

I?" – jokes with the audience, plunging us into an unfamiliar world of philosophical confusion about the nature of being (Act 1). Does Estragon, in fact, exist at all? Our uncertainty is increased further as they begin to discuss the fact that Estragon has spent the night in a ditch, being beaten by a group of people. Who are these people? Why are they hurting him?

Beckett's stage set raises more questions. It is intentionally minimal. The road is the empty stage itself, its only ornaments are a leafless tree and a "low mound", which was changed by Beckett to a rectangular stone in later productions. It is, in short, a play in which, as critic Vivien Mercier famously said: "Nothing happens twice" – in Act 1 and then again in Act 2.

Did Beckett intend the play to fail?

Such a drama does not seem designed to thrill an audience. But Beckett didn't mind if his productions flopped. He decided to ask the French actor-director Roger Blin to take on the first production of Godot, partly because Blin's previous production had been commercially unsuccessful. Blin may not have been crowd-pleasing, but, for Beckett, a director who would not sacrifice artistic integrity for audience numbers was a find.

Blin had to wait three years to get the funds together and *En Attendant Godot* was first performed at the Théatre de Babylone, Paris, on 5th January, 1953.

The reaction was mixed. One of the original actors claimed that the first night was "the theatre event of the world". However, the cast had to put up with criticism. At one performance, the curtain even had to be dropped early, as the audience hooted and whistled their way through Lucky's extraordinary, incomprehensible monologue. Soon, however, murmurs of approval spread, and with the public's appetite for controversy, Beckett's play became the must-see show of Paris's Left Bank, spawning versions in Spanish and German that same year.

Concerned that somebody would soon attempt a poor, pirated English translation, Beckett quickly set about the job himself, and Peter Hall's British production opened in London in August 1955. Although two reviewers found it exceptional, the play was not well received. As Peter Bull, the actor who played Pozzo, said: "Waves of hostility came whirling over the footlights, and the mass exodus, which was to form such a feature of the run of the piece, started quite soon after the curtain had risen. The audible groans were also fairly disconcerting." Audiences in America were equally difficult to please. Director Alan Schneider wrote to Beckett to apologise for his disastrous production in Miami, in which a large number of the audience walked out. Beckett told Schneider that he wasn't disappointed. Failure, it seems, was part of the way in which he thought about art. He had, he claimed, "breathed deep" of its "vivifying air" for his entire career.

Most audiences, of course, expect to be a little disorientated at the beginning of a dramatic production. They are used, perhaps, to being initially confused about the location, the relationship between the characters, and the plot. However, they expect that all will soon be revealed, and that their efforts will be rewarded by a story that makes sense. But in Beckett's play, no such revelations take place. In this manner, *Waiting for Godot* struck its first audiences as a scandalous dramatic outrage. Many of his audiences in the 1950s, and many readers today, still expect what was known in the 19th and early 20th century as a "well-made play" – one which will quickly set up the relationships between the characters and establish the story so far, offering a climax, a denouement, and, most importantly, a moral.

This may be what tradition demands, but, as Vladimir remarks at the end of the play, "habit is a great deadener" (Act 2). If we are to adopt Hamlet's idea that a play holds up a mirror to nature, then a "well-made play" implies that reality is, in important ways, well-made. It suggests that the world, like the play, has a plot, a moral, and is shaped according to some design. In playing with Shakespeare's thoughts on dramatic mimesis, Beckett offers his audience a new kind of world, shaking them out of their habitual, deadened modes of thought.

Though perfectly constructed, *Waiting For Godot* defies our conventional expectations of theatre-going. Beckett claimed that if it was performed the way that he desired, it "would empty the theatre". The comment can be read in two ways. Beckett might be suggesting his drama is so complex and difficult that people would want to leave before the interval; or he might be suggesting that if they stayed they would be given the sense that the idea of theatre itself has been hollowed out, emptied of its potency, and of its gravitas. Emptied, perhaps, of everything but its humour.

How funny is *Waiting for Godot*?

One thing often forgotten in critical discussions of *Waiting for Godot* is the fact that the play is very funny. While at University in Dublin, Beckett frequently attended Vaudeville theatre, and loved watching the films of Chaplin, Laurel and Hardy and Harold Lloyd. The influence of their slapstick antics is clearly evident in Godot, and recent productions have frequently cast comedians in the lead roles, from Rik Mayall and Adrian Edmonson to Robin Williams and Steve Martin. Vladimir and Estragon seem oddly and comically, similar, both dressed like tramps, with matching bowler hats. They are, however, distinguished by their specific health complaints. Vladimir has some sort of problem with his prostate gland, causing a weak bladder. As a result, he becomes, quite literally, a running joke over the course of the play, frequently ducking towards the exit to relieve himself Estragon, meanwhile, is preoccupied with taking off his boots because he has problems with his feet. Pain, however, brings them into a strange kind of harmony.

ESTRAGON:
　[Feebly.] Help me!
VLADIMIR:
　It hurts?
ESTRAGON:
　Hurts! He wants to know if it hurts!
VLADIMIR
　[Angrily.] No one ever suffers but you. I don't count. I'd like to hear what you'd say if you had what I have.
ESTRAGON:
　It hurts?
VLADIMIR:
　Hurts! He wants to know if it hurts! (Act 1)

In *Waiting for Godot* laughter often coincides with pain, indignity or obscenity. Take the combination of scatological and slapstick humour when Vladimir is told that his trouser fly is still undone, or Estragon's excitement when he hears that he might get an erection from hanging himself. Such moments jostle with more complex forms of verbal humour, as when Vladimir ponders why he waits until the last moment before going to the toilet:

> VLADIMIR:
> *[Musingly.] The last moment ... [He meditates.] Hope deferred maketh the something sick, who said that?*
> ESTRAGON:
> *Why don't you help me?*
> VLADIMIR:
> *Sometimes I feel it coming all the same. Then I go all queer ... How shall I say ... Relieved and at the same time ... appalled. (Act 1)*

As in most of Beckett's prose and dramatic works, the gags are clever. A subtle pun on the idea of physical relief (emptying the bladder) and emotional relief (getting off-stage in time) is woven into a biblical reference. Here, Vladimir puts a comic twist on Proverbs 13: 12: "Hope deferred makes the heart sick: but when desire cometh it is the tree of life." Early audiences commented that Vladimir and Estragon's biblical banterings resembled a weary, well-worn comic routine.

Elsewhere, the comedy is dark. At the moment, for instance, when the abused and downtrodden

A performance of Waiting for Godot *at the Theatre Royal, Bath, in 2005*

Lucky begins to cry, the audience might begin to wonder quite what species of drama they are watching. Estragon goes over to Lucky to wipe away his tears, but Lucky returns this gesture by kicking him violently in the shins. This sudden switch from compassion to brutality seems both comic and disturbing. Beckett's note that he is writing in the hybrid genre of tragi-comedy should be borne in mind here. Laughter, as the French philosopher Henri Bergson wrote, can immunise us to pain – it provides "a momentary anaesthesia of the heart".

Humans or animals?

The most painful elements of the play concern the characters of Lucky and Pozzo. Quite different from the symbiotic – and sometimes companionable – pairing of Estragon and Vladimir, Pozzo appears to be the master to Lucky's slave. Lucky enters first on a leash, driven by Pozzo's whip and his cries of "On!". Estragon and Vladimir are at first mystified by the relationship between the pair, then appalled, as they note the running sore around Lucky's neck, caused by the rope. Why, both they and the audience are forced to ask, does Pozzo treat Lucky like an animal? Why would anyone continue to endure such a tyrannical command, and what will be done about it?

This grotesque scene is, however, pierced with comedy as Vladimir and Estragon wonder, initially, if Pozzo is the long-awaited Godot, initiating a wrangle over names. But the various confusions of "Bozzo", "Pozzo" and the figure of "Godot" (who Pozzo soon refers to "Godet ... Godot ...Godin") are not merely comic (Act 1). They show the way in which names, the most certain signifiers of self-definition, seem to be losing their meaning in this world. Soon, the idea of self-definition becomes even more confusing, as Pozzo assures himself that Estragon and Vladimir are at least "human beings none the less" and "of the same species" as himself. It may seem an odd assurance, but by this point in the play, quite what species any of these characters are seems uncertain. While Pozzo sets about eating his chicken "voraciously, throwing away the bones", Vladimir and Estragon seem to be having trouble in classifying Lucky, as he stands, leash around his head, holding Pozzo's bags. While they settle on the possibility that "he's a cretin" or "a half-wit", his degraded state leaves Vladimir uncertain as to whether he is a "man" or not, as the hesitation in his outburst shows:

VLADIMIR:
 To treat a man ... [Gesture towards LUCKY] ... like that ... I think that ... no ... a human being ... no ... it's a scandal.
ESTRAGON:
 [Not to be outdone.] A disgrace!
 [He resumes his gnawing.]

Despite Pozzo's exaggerated politeness, his treatment of Lucky appears to lack the features of what we might define as basic humanity. As Pozzo himself airily admits, he is "not particularly human". Recently, critics such as Shane Weller and Mary Bryden have written perceptively about Beckett's interest in the animal world, and the idea of "shared subjection" between the two and the four-legged beings in his work. The dubious relationship between man and animal displayed in this scene runs through the play, rippling out to the audience and their own conceptions of selfhood.

Who is Godot?

The figure that has proved most challenging for audiences and readers to define is the one that never turns up. Who is Godot? What is he? Are we meant to think he actually exists? The identity of Godot is never made clear. Estragon admits he "wouldn't know him" if he saw him, nor can Vladimir or Estragon remember what they asked him for. That said, the semantic richness of his name, along with the recollection that they have formerly addressed him with a "kind of prayer" invites various allegorical explanations (Act 1). In answer to the actor Jack MacGowran, Beckett was emphatic in denying the most popular theory about Godot: "Because Godot begins with g-o-d, people have got the idea that he's referring to God. But he categorically states that that is not the point at all, that it doesn't mean God at all." That said, Beckett tempts the religious interpretation, always emphasising that the word should be pronounced with the emphasis on the first syllable.

Theology does haunt this play. Although he professed no religion, Beckett was brought up in a strict Protestant background and the Bible would have been part of his everyday vocabulary. Throughout the script there are references to the scriptures - moments in which the words of the Bible are half-remembered and half-forgotten. In Beckett's world, sacred discourse, like all language, is revealed to be unreliable, and infinitely forgettable. Elsewhere, we find the idea of the crucifixion reduced to a cliché – as Vladimir sighs "To every many his little cross", or to a parody, as when Estragon attempts to do a yoga exercise called "the tree" (Act 2).

Elsewhere, the characters carry each other, paralleling images of Calvary and Christ's descent from the cross. Such sacred resonances invite one to read the play as if it were, in some sense, a religious allegory. Beckett resisted such readings, commenting simply that Christianity "is a mythology with which I am perfectly familiar, so naturally I use it". Like all the allusions in the play, references to the scripture set up echoes to common memories, making the audience think about what has been lost.

Later, Beckett joked with the director Alan Schneider that the name derived from the French slang for various kinds of boots ("godillot" or "godasses"). Overall, Beckett encouraged a proliferation of interpretations of "Godot", but resisted explanation. When asked "Who or what does Godot mean?" he replied: "If I knew, I would have said so in the play." Perhaps the one thing that we can be certain about is that "Godot" offers the reader and audience the same experience of not knowing, waiting, and questioning, that pervades the entire play, captured by the repetitive refrain:

> *ESTRAGON:*
>   *Let's go.*
> *VLADIMIR:*
>   *We can't.*
> *ESTRAGON:*
>   *Why not?*
> *VLADIMIR:*
>   *We're waiting for Godot.*
> *ESTRAGON:*
>   *[Despairingly.] Ah! (Acts 1 and 2)*

Why are Beckett's stage directions so precise?

Vladimir's famous line – "We're waiting for Godot" – can also be read as a comment about theatre. The actors cannot leave the stage because they are waiting for Godot – they make up the substance of the play's title. While neither of these players seems sure what they are doing on this stage, they are agonisingly aware of a need to continue to perform, as when Vladimir urges Estragon to "return the ball" of their dialogue (Act 1). Sometimes, it seems, the performance becomes too much for them. When Estragon attempts to get

Vladimir to tell a formulaic dirty story about an Englishman in a brothel, Vladimir's response is to shout for him to stop. The argument implies that the pair have been performing the same routine and telling the same jokes like two worn-out comedians in a run that never has a last night. Elsewhere, they comment upon the play's action, like a pair of disgruntled critics:

> *ESTRAGON:*
> *It's awful.*
> *VLADIMIR:*
> *Worse than the pantomime.*
> *ESTRAGON:*
> *The circus.*
> *VLADIMIR:*
> *The music-hall.*
> *ESTRAGON:*
> *The circus. (Act 1)*

Conventionally, when watching a play, the playwright aims to get the audience to collaborate with them in what Coleridge refers to as "a willing suspension of disbelief"; to forget that they are watching a play and to pretend, for the performance, that the world they are viewing is "real". Throughout *Waiting For Godot*, however, the characters purposely sabotage the realism of their own play. Vladimir and Estragon, for instance, draw attention to their theatrical environment, as when Estragon looks out at the "inspiring prospects" of the audience (Act 1). His later comment – "Nobody comes, nobody goes. It's awful!" – could be taken as an apposite commentary on the play itself. Indeed, the playwright Jean Anouilh used these very words after seeing the 1953 première of the play. Estragon's lament begs a question, though. Why are the characters continuing to "act", if they are aware that their performance is so terribly shoddy? As with the play as a whole, there is no answer, but there is perhaps a hint, in the fact that all these figures are under another tyrannical command: they are following a script.

For those reading the text, rather than viewing the play, they will notice that it contains numerous detailed, italicised commands. Beckett commented that he started to write *Waiting for Godot* because he wanted to work in a medium where he had "control of where people stood or moved". This control is evident throughout. When Lucky puts down Pozzo's bag or helps him off with his coat, or when Pozzo sits down and eats a chicken lunch, every action is carefully choreographed by Beckett.

Such attention to detail is characteristic of his drama. As the Beckettian actress and critic Rosemary Pountney remarks, "no playwright has more exacting stage directions than Beckett", and he was fierce with directors who tried to change *Godot*'s staging. If art is a mirror of life, then Beckett's mirror suggests that we live in a world in which we are forced to perform to a pre-ordained script. Some stage directions, like the complex manoeuvrings between Lucky and Pozzo, are difficult for the actors to carry out. Others, like the extraordinary moment when Vladimir is directed to "[use his intelligence]" (Act 1) are near impossible. It is tempting to see Beckett's stage-directing voice as analogous to an indifferent, higher power. To suggest, however, that Beckett's play is drawing direct parallels between the artist and God is to go against his own principles of interpretation. Nevertheless, the power of what Beckett termed his "cold eye" forces us to think, and thinking, as Lucky goes on to show, is a dangerous thing.

What is Beckett telling us about life?

The character suffering under the most dramatic constraints is, of course, Pozzo's servant Lucky. In terms of the plot, Pozzo himself stages Lucky's entire existence. Meanwhile, the actor playing this part is required to memorise nearly two pages of incomprehensible monologue. The director of the first Dublin production remembers that his Lucky was nearly overwhelmed by the sheer enormity of the task. The monologue in question is, of course, performed at Pozzo's command, forcing him to "think" for their entertainment. Beckett was reported to require that Lucky's speech be "like a phonograph record getting faster and faster and faster until it is out of control" – a feat of delivery that would ask a great deal of any actor.

When Pozzo suggests this brand of diversion, Estragon and Vladimir are taken aback:

> POZZO:
> *[He picks up the whip.] What do you prefer? Shall we have him dance, or sing, or recite, or think, or –*
> ESTRAGON:
> *Who?*
> POZZO:
> *Who! You know how to think, you two?*
> VLADIMIR:
> *He thinks?*
> POZZO:
> *Certainly. Aloud. He even used to think very prettily once, I could listen to him for hours. (Act 1)*

The cause of Vladimir's surprise is left uncertain. Is he shocked that "thinking" is seen as a form of entertainment, that it can be performed on command, or is he surprised because thinking is an activity that Vladimir or Estragon have forgotten about? As Lucky begins his tirade of incomprehensible prose, Beckett draws his audience's attention to a paradox. For if one is "ordered" to "think", the suggestion is that one is obeying, rather than thinking.

The speech that follows, lacking in any punctuation or conventional grammar, was of great importance to Beckett. He chose it as the starting point when rehearsing the production in Berlin in 1975. Despite its apparent nonsensicality, Beckett claimed that it could be divided into three parts, and the second of these parts fell into two sections:

> The first part is about the indifference of heaven, about divine apathy. This part ends with "but not so fast ...". The second part starts off with "considering what is more", and is about man, who is shrinking – man who is dwindling. Not only the dwindling is important here, but the shrinking, too. These two points represents the two under sections of the second part. The theme of the third part is "the earth abode of stones" and starts with "considering what is more, much more grave".

Lucky begins by wondering about the existence of a God who has a white beard and is compassionate, rather like Miranda, the heroine of Shakespeare's *The Tempest*. However, there is something forgetful about this God. He suffers from "athambia", which denotes an imperturbability about those around him, "aphasia", the loss of the ability to speak or write, and "apathia" which results in little concern for those around him. For "reasons unknown" to Lucky, he loves all of humanity deeply "with some exceptions". At this point the speech dives down into the idea of what happens to those "exceptions" who are "plunged in torment", and consumed with fire and brimstone. He then moves on to the idea that despite the progress that man has made – what Lucky terms "the strides of alimentation and defecation" – and all the various activities man undertakes, we can be seen to "shrink and dwindle". He finishes with a morbid lament on the state of man, reflecting on skull and stones. One can tenuously link Lucky's reference to the skull with Golgotha, the site of Christ's crucifixion. Beckett, meanwhile, noted that the speech is "all about stones, about the world of stones", as if emphasising that he was speaking about the most basic elements of existence.

At around the mid-point of Lucky's enigmatic speech, which he claims to give "in brief", there is a mention of Bishop Berkeley, an 18th-century churchman and philosopher. George Berkeley wrote about the nature of existence, arguing that matter only existed if it was perceived, and the world existed because it was seen by God. This argument, contained in his most famous observation – " esse est percipi" ("to be is to be perceived") – haunts much of Beckett's work, including *Waiting for Godot*. However, while Lucky's speech seems to be pondering such questions about philosophy and metaphysics, it is also a parody of such philosophical thinking. In the style of an academic giving an account of his research, Lucky repeatedly alludes to imaginary texts and scholars to back up his points. Some such as "Testew and Cunard", or "Fartov and Belcher" are crude puns. Elsewhere, Lucky makes joking references to concerns about man's existence. "Essy-in-Possy", for instance, the location of Lucky's fictional Academy, picks up on the Latin for "being" and "being able" – "esse" and "posse"

While Lucky leans on the language of scholarly argument, especially its use of formal conjunctions such as "hereinafter" and "what is more", the sense of his own argument seems to be falling apart. The strange stammering of "quaquaquaqua", a failed attempt to say "quaversalis", meaning "in all directions a the same time" gives the impression that his speech has become stuck in a groove. Lucky's grip on language seems to be slipping, as he clings to the remnants of his argument, and finally finishes, "unfinished". In choosing to present the play's main "philosophical" argument in an incomprehensible, fragmentary, comic form, Beckett seems to be suggesting to his audience that thoughts about existence are beyond speech. Language cannot offer us a route to truth. As he wrote in a letter to his friend Axel Kaun a decade earlier, "my own language appears to me like a veil that must be torn apart in order to get at the things (or the Nothingness) behind it".

Why is repetition so important in the play?

The beginning of Act Two was a risky business when the play was originally performed. In the first Paris production, a group of the audience made a sensation by exiting en masse when the curtain opened on the same scene of two men, waiting under a tree. This was a shame, because they were destined to miss a certain beauty in this replay. In a 1931 essay about Proust, Beckett praised the novelistic technique of repetition, making a comparison with "the beautiful convention of da capo" in musical composition, in which a musician is directed to return to the beginning of a section of music, and repeat.

While it may be pleasing when encountered on a small-scale, Beckett's use of repetition in *Waiting for Godot* has a more powerful and disturbing effect. As the literary theorist Ihab Hassan points out, it only takes two acts to suggest an infinite sequence of recurring, identical scenes. The implication is that, perhaps, we are witnessing an excerpt from a play that has an infinite number of acts, each the same as the next. This sense of infinite repetition is heightened by Beckett's teasing introduction of an actual "da capo", Vladimir's song about "the dog" which "came into the kitchen", which can be repeated for an eternity.

As they resume their discussion, Vladimir becomes increasingly alarmed that Estragon claims not to remember the actions of the previous act. Only under pressure does he recall Pozzo and Lucky, and cannot remember when their last meeting took place. Estragon's forgetfulness is unsettling, but perhaps comprehensible. If the pair is being forced to repeat the same actions from day to day (like actors in an endless run) then maybe it is better not to be conscious of the repetition. Indeed, as the duo's dialogue proceeds, they appear to fall into a purgatorial circular linguistic dynamic, in which Estragon can only repeat himself:

ESTRAGON:
  All the dead voices.
VLADIMIR:
  They make a noise like wings.
ESTRAGON:
  Like leaves.
VLADIMIR:
  Like sand.
ESTRAGON:
  Like leaves. (Act 2)

The idea of life as an eternal repetition bears a relation to a famous essay written in 1941 by the existential philosopher Albert Camus, which compares man's condition to the Greek myth of

Sisyphus. Sisyphus was a man who was condemned to perform the same action, of rolling a rock up a hill, only for it to roll down again, eternally. The concept of repetition can be both comforting, and terrifying. Small-scale refrains, like the lullaby that Vladimir later sings to Estragon, or the habitual give-and-take of daily routine can be comforting, and they help us to confirm our identity. The idea of infinite repetition seems less easy. If life is simply played on repeat, one suspects that it may lose its authenticity or significance, like the historical events that Karl Marx famously said happen twice, first as tragedy, and then again as farce.

While Beckett's characters appear to be caught in the same plight as Sisyphus, their treatment is less tragic. It is lightened, in part, by Beckett's almost blasé opening stage direction - "Next Day. Same Time. Same Place" – which seems to suggest that the Sisyphyan existential dilemma is itself a little old hat. What is more, as the second act reveals, there are subtle and mysterious differences in their environment – a growth of leaves on the tree, and a different pair of boots beneath it.

Does Beckett mock the idea of human solidarity?

Once Vladimir and Estragon have established that today, is, indeed, slightly different from yesterday, Estragon proceeds to try on the new pair of boots that have appeared under the tree. His discovery that they fit has echoes of the Cinderella fairytale about it, but it also chimes with another proverbial commonplace – the old adage of a person putting themselves in somebody else's shoes, of trying to understand what it is like to be to be another person.

Over the next few minutes, Estragon and Vladimir play with ideas of other people. First they swap hats in a parodic vaudeville. Then they try "playing at being Pozzo and Lucky". While their posturings, echoing Pozzo's vicious nature and Lucky's bereft drooping are mocking, they also show the characters reaching towards a position of understanding. This same tonal ambivalence underlies their melodramatic calls for divine justice, as they both pretend to pray, and desperately plead for help:

ESTRAGON:
　God have pity on me!
VLADIMIR:
　[Vexed.] And me?
ESTRAGON:
　On me! On me! Pity! On me! (Act 2)

FIVE FACTS ABOUT BECKETT & *WAITING FOR GODOT*

1. Samuel Beckett is the only Nobel literature laureate to have played first-class cricket. He played twice for Dublin University in first-class fixtures, against Northamptonshire in 1925 and 1926.

2. Following his work with the French Resistance during World War Two, Beckett was awarded the Croix de Guerre. On two occasions he was nearly caught by the Gestapo but would always make light of his wartime exploits in later life, referring to them as "boy scout stuff".

3. Beckett knew little about the theatre when he started writing. It was only through attending rehearsals of his own plays during the 1950s that he came to understand it properly.

4. Peter Hall directed the premiere of the English language version of the play in 1955 at the Arts Theatre in London. Theatre critic Kenneth Tynan said the performance "changed the rules of theatre".

5. The American children's television show *Sesame Street* dedicated an episode to the play in 1996. "Waiting for Elmo" featured characters Grover and Telly Monster waiting endlessly at a dead tree. Elmo didn't turn up.

Opposite: Ian McKellen as Estagon and Patrick Stewart as Vladimir in Sean Mathias's 2009 production of Waiting for Godot *at The Royal Theatre Haymarket, London*

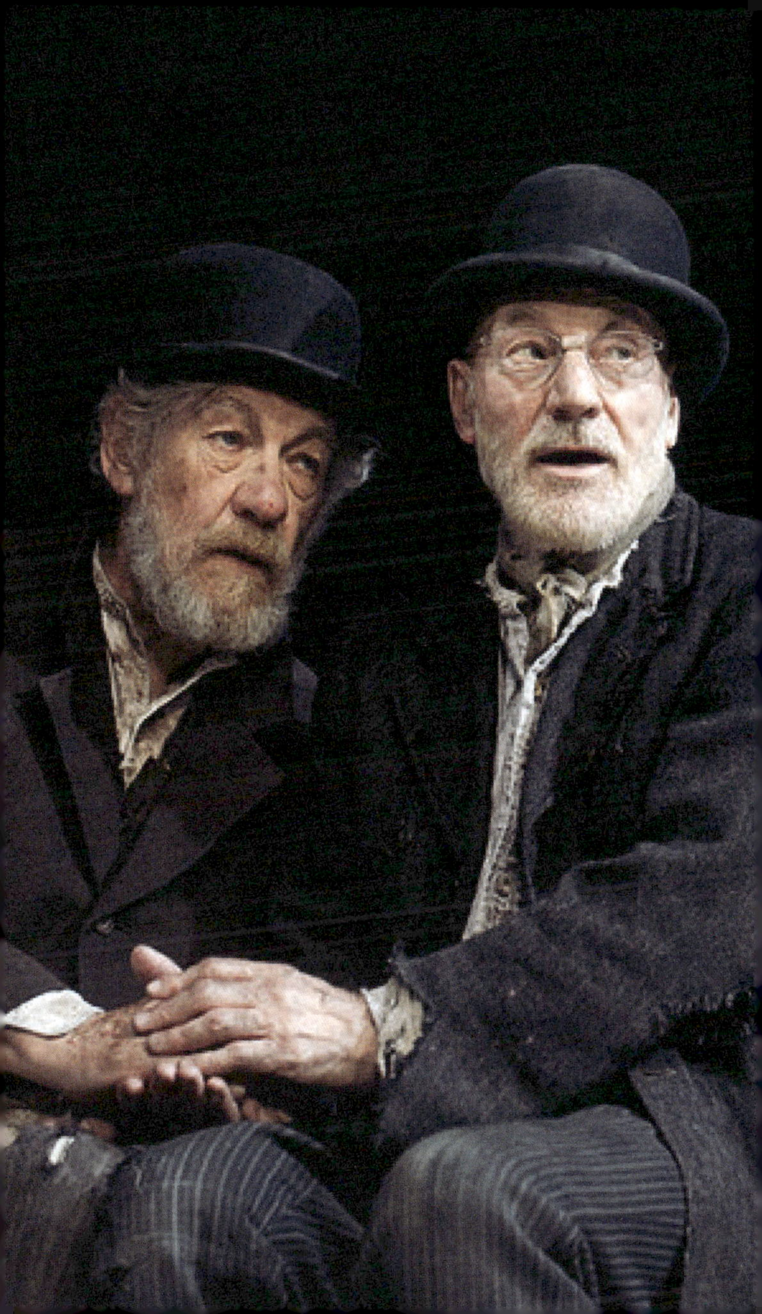

The figure of Pozzo, re-entering the stage, interrupts their outburst, and his blinded figure recalls the stuff of Greek tragedy. Like Sophocles's Oedipus, or Shakespeare's Gloucester in *King Lear*, he seems to ask for the audience's and the protagonists's pity, as he falls down on the stage and is unable to find his feet. His plight, however, is followed by a long debate between Vladimir and Estragon as to whether or not they should come to his aid. Questions of human solidarity, help, and sympathy run through this section of the play. Indeed, Beckett highlighted the idea of "Help" in his notebooks about the production of *Waiting for Godot*, noting that there are 21 instances in which one of his protagonists asks for help – and only 14 are answered.

Understanding and compassion was not something that Beckett thought came easily to humanity. Pain, he commented in his essay on Proust, "can only be focussed at a distance". This view has led some critics to perceive his drama as inhumane. In fact, what he does show is how difficult it is for people to achieve a truly humane understanding of each other. While Pozzo lies, crying for help, Vladimir sets off on a tour de force of rhetorical flourishes and self-congratulation in an attempt to urge Estragon into some sort of action. While he claims that they should not "waste ... time in idle discourse", this is precisely what he does:

> *It is not every day that we are needed. Not indeed that we personally are needed. Others would meet the case equally well, if not better. To all mankind they were addressed, those cries for help still ringing in our ears!*

But at this place, at this moment in time, all mankind is us, whether we like it or not. (Act 2)

Beckett picks up on the irony of Vladimir's pose. While he enjoys the idea of human solidarity, he is only considering it as a theoretical possibility, taking what T. S. Eliot refers to as the aesthetic rather than the moral attitude to life. Beckett slyly signposts Vladimir's speech for us, showing us that we are to take his compassion with a pinch of salt by giving him dramatic stage-directions and overly metaphorical language. He even turns him, for a moment, into a parodic tragic hero. Vladimir's "What are we doing here, that is the question" (Act 2) sends the audience back to that most famous of literary procrastinators – Hamlet the Dane ("To be, or not to be: that is the question"). When they do finally help Pozzo, Vladimir and Estragon both end up on the stage floor as well.

In making the idea of giving someone a helping hand so farcically difficult, Beckett once again suggests that helping people may not be as easy as convention dictates. What Beckett is mocking here is not the idea of human solidarity. He mocks those who try to make solidarity sound easy. It's a provocative message to explore in a world trying to recover after international war.

What should we make of the "climax"?

Anton Chekhov, another great writer of tragicomedy, pointed up the way in which playwrights conventionally structure their dramas. If, he noted, "there is a gun hanging on the wall in the first act, it must fire in the last". The ending of *Godot*, as with much of Chekhov, brings nothing so explosive. The boy returns, to inform them that Mr Godot "won't come this evening". What is worse, he appears to have no recollection of Vladimir, or his previous visit, referring to him, again, as "Mr Albert". In place of a classical scene of recognition, or anagnorisis, Vladimir meets a blank. Vladimir tries to make sense of the fact that the boy does not recognise him, suggesting, perhaps, that the boy has a brother who came the day before, but to no avail. Things are no easier for the audience. As the cast list notes that there is only one 'Boy', are we to assume that this is the same figure as the goat-herder in Act One, or is the character playing a double role? The conversation increases Vladimir's sense of anxiety about his tenuous existence:

Samuel Beckett at a rehearsal of Waiting for Godot *at The Royal Court Theatre, London, in 1976*

BOY:
　　What am I to tell Mr Godot, sir?

VLADIMIR:
　　Tell him ... [He hesitates]...tell him you saw me and that ... [He hesitates] ... that you saw me. [Pause. VLADIMIR advances, the BOY recoils. VLADIMIR halts, the BOY halts. With sudden violence.] You're sure you saw me, you won't come and tell me tomorrow that you never saw me! (Act 2)

This appeal has a history. In Act One, Vladimir has asked the same boy "You did see us, didn't you?", and Vladimir's need for confirmation that their meeting has taken place is entwined with the problem of whether one's existence is governed by being perceived.

As the final act draws to its close, and Estragon and Vladimir contemplate what they are to do, and whether they should, at last, hang themselves, Beckett provides his audience with a final, brilliant, comic sadness. Lacking a noose to finish the job off, they wonder whether Estragon's belt will do the trick. "It might do at a pinch," Vladimir considers. "But is it strong enough?" (Act 2). As they each take an end of the cord and pull, the rope-belt breaks. Recovering from their tug-of war, "They almost fall". "Almost", like "perhaps", is a key-word for Beckett. Estragon confesses to Vladimir that he, too, "can't go on like this" – but while the two figures are in the depths of despair, they have not quite fallen. Something else does though. Perfecting the art of tragic bathos, the final descent is not of humanity, but of a pair of beltless trousers.

Beckett was very particular about the trousers. He was concerned to hear that in the French première of the show, Estragon kept them halfway up, and wrote to Roger Blin to make sure that they fell completely around the character's ankles. Beckett admitted that such attention to detail must seem silly, but following Estragon's advice, he never neglects the "little things" (Act 1).

It is little things like the poetic reversal at the

close of Act Two that give the play its power. Beckett's entrances and exits act, for the characters, and, perhaps, for the audience, as rehearsals of their final leave-taking. In this sense, *Waiting for Godot* offers a sensitivity to the simultaneous longing for closure, and desire for continuance, that haunts every life, and every good piece of art. This time it is Vladimir who suggests "Let's go". Once again "they do not move" (Act 2). One cannot fail to be moved.

Does *Waiting for Godot* belong to the 'Theatre of the Absurd'?

Echoes of *Waiting for Godot* persist throughout Beckett's writing life, creeping into his later works. The concerns of Vladimir and Estragon, Pozzo and Lucky, find themselves played out, again and again, in his later prose. But the play also finds what Beckett referred to in his novel *Mercier and Camier* as a "life of afterlife" elsewhere, influencing both his contemporaries (Edward Albee, Harold Pinter, Sam Shepard) and the next generation of writers for stage and screen, such as Sarah Kane, Tom Stoppard, David Mamet, and Quentin Tarantino.

The play has been critically influential too. As William Hutchings notes, only Shakespeare's *Hamlet* can lay claim a greater number and variety of critical readings. But negotiating a critical stance with which to approach *Waiting For Godot* is tricky. Beckett directs us to treat any critical stance with a dose of scepticism. It is worth remembering that when he is exchanging insults with Vladimir, "Crritic!" is the worst insult that Estragon can summon (Act 1). *Waiting for Godot* is Beckett notes, "a play which was striving all the time to avoid definition".

Definitions are, however, constantly attempted by critics. Beckett's *Godot* has been aligned by Martin Esslin with works by a group of playwrights writing in Europe just after the Second World War, such as Eugene Ionesco, Antoine Artaud and Jean-Paul Sartre. These works, which Esslin termed the 'Theatre of the Absurd', might be said to share a common disillusionment with the times in which their authors lived, and an anxiety about the nature of religion, politics, identity, responsibility and language. Sartre was also a philosopher, and much absurdist drama is related to the concerns of the existential philosophy that he espoused. For the existentialists, individuals are trapped in a dilemma in which they are forced to act without a secure sense of the external world, reality, universally accepted moral criteria, or any omnipotent being such as God. The playwrights who were influenced by this philosophy set about using theatrical form to examine the idea that existence itself was futile and senseless, characteristically playing with theatrical conventions and offering dreamless, nonsensical, reflexive dramas.

While Beckett's dramatic world seems to share features of absurdism, Esslin is wrong to place him so firmly in this category. As Beckett noted himself, his drama is "not about philosophy, but about situations", while the French director Roger Blin claimed that Beckett had "no ideas – no theories – on theatre at all".

Why argue so strongly against the idea of Beckett as an existentialist, or a practitioner of the 'Theatre of the Absurd'? Because existentialist philosophy has some element of coherence about it, evident in the very fact that it can even be characterised as a "philosophy". Sartre held on to the possibility that individuals could force their own philosophical meaning out of a situation of meaninglessness. This is reflected in his own drama, in which characters hold philosophical positions, and seem to urge the audience to reconsider, act, and take responsibility. While Beckett read many philosophers in great depth, including Descartes, Pascal, Schopenhauer and Kierkegaard, his texts approach philosophical stances with scepticism, and continually parody the condition that might be seen as existential angst. As the critic Theodor Adorno notes, in Beckett's world philosophy itself proclaims its "bankruptcy".

One must perhaps look closer to home, in the attempt to understand or place Beckett's *Godot*. While he wrote in post-war Paris, the play clearly shows his Irish heritage. The tramps on the roadside echo the tinkers and beggars inhabiting Synge's turn-of-the-century Irish tragedies which Beckett had seen in the Abbey Theatre in Dublin. Meanwhile, the play adapts and draws on numerous other literary models. The Greek tragedians, Shakespeare and Racine are all woven into its complex texture. The thoughts of philosophers such as Wittgenstein, Heidegger, Saussure and Derrida jostle among them.

For other critics, *Waiting for Godot* can be seen as an example of the way in which modernist drama stands on the threshold of the postmodern. Rather than asking modernist "epistemological" questions about how we interpret the world, the play seems to be concerned with postmodern "ontological" worries – worries about which world we might be in, and whether what we might see as our common reality matters at all. In facing Beckett's drama, an audience is asked to consider multiple worlds, and to wonder whether the "world" of *Waiting for Godot* bears any relation to their own. The resulting text communicates (or fails to communicate) undecidability and openness.

Recent critical responses have been most successful when they cease to "define" Beckett's drama and look at how it works, or feels. Ulrika

Maude, for instance, discusses the ways in which *Godot* is experienced by an audience's senses. It is a play, Beckett argued, which helps an audience to feel "not only themes in the script, but themes in the body". Indeed, perhaps the best way of coming closer to understanding *Waiting for Godot* is to see and feel a good production. This experience is not necessarily an easy one. Beckett was always careful to tell his directors that they should "bore the audience". The effect, and the influence, of the drama depends, primarily, on the experience of waiting, and of struggling with this emptiness.

Among the many anecdotes and tales of engagements with Beckett, one stands out. In 1957, a group of actors from San Francisco had visited the notoriously tough San Quentin State Prison. They had chosen to perform *Waiting for Godot*, in part, because it had no women in it, and was therefore suitable for the all-male confines of San Quentin. The cast was nervous as the curtain rose, but as the critic Martin Esslin notes, what "bewildered the sophisticated audiences of Paris, London and New York was immediately grasped by an audience of convicts". One among the audience, Rick Cluchey, went on to write himself, and later became close friends with Beckett. Even within a prison, it seems, *Waiting for Godot* managed to open doors.

A SHORT CHRONOLOGY

1906 April 13 Beckett born in Foxrock, near Dublin

1927 After studying for a degree in Modern Languages at Trinity College, Dublin, Beckett moves to Paris, where he works as a lecteur

1931 Beckett returns to Dublin, as an assistant lecturer at Trinity College, and his first piece of literary criticism, a book on Proust, is published

1932-1937 Beckett moves back to Paris. After much travelling, he settles there for good

1938 Beckett stabbed in the chest and nearly killed by a French Pimp called 'Prudent'. His first novel, *Murphy*, is published

1940 Hitler invades France. Beckett joins the Resistance and moves from Paris to the South of France in 1942 to escape the Gestapo

1946-1953 Back in Paris, Beckett writes a trilogy of novels - *Molloy, Malone Dies, The Unnameable* - and Waiting for Godot

1953 *Waiting for Godot* premieres in Paris

1955 First production of *Godot* in London

1969 Beckett awarded the Nobel Prize for Literature

1989 December 22 Beckett dies

FURTHER READING

WORKS OF SAMUEL BECKETT
Proust, London: Chatto & Windus, 1931
Waiting for Godot, London: Faber, 1965
Molloy: Malone Dies: The Unnamable, London: Calder & Boyers, 1966

SECONDARY LITERATURE
Abbott, H. Porter, *Beckett Writing Beckett; the Author in the Autograph*, Ithaca: Cornell University Press, 1996.

Adorno, Theodor W, 'Trying to Understand Endgame' in *Samuel Beckett's 'Endgame'*, ed. Harold Bloom. New York: New Haven: Chelsea House, 1988.

Andonian, Cathleen Culotta (ed.), *The Critical Response to Samuel Beckett*. London: Greenwood Press, 1998.

Asmus, Walter, 'Beckett Directs Godot', *Theatre Quarterly*, 5 (September, November 1975), pp. 19-26.

Bair, Deirdre, *Samuel Beckett: A Biography*. London: Vintage, 1990.

Bloom, Harold, (ed.) *Samuel Beckett's Waiting for Godot: Modern Critical Interpretations*. New

York: Chelsea House, 1987.

Busi, Frederick, *The Transformations of Godot*. Lexington: University Press of Kentucky, 1980.

Cohn, Ruby (ed.), *Samuel Beckett: A collection of Criticism.* New York: McGraw, 1975.

Cohn, Ruby. *Just Play: Beckett's Theater*, Princeton, New Jersey: Princeton University Press, 1980

Cohn, Ruby (ed.), *Waiting for Godot: A Casebook*. London: Macmillan, 1987

Connor, Steven (ed.), *Waiting for Godot and Endgame*, London: Macmillan, 1992

Driver, Tom, "Beckett by The Madelaine", *Columbia University Forum IV*, Summer 1961

Esslin, Martin, *The Theater of the Absurd*.1961; rev. edn., Harmondsworth: Penguin, 1968.

Fletcher, Beryl, et al. *A Student's Guide to the Plays of Samuel Beckett*, London: Chatto and Windus, 1967

Gordon, Lois, *Reading Godot*. New Haven and London: Yale University Press, 2002

Graver, Lawrence, *Waiting for Godot* Cambridge: Cambridge University Press, 1989

Harmon, Maurice.(ed.), *No Author Better Served: the Correspondence of Samuel Beckett and Alan Schneider.* Cambridge; Mass.: Harvard University Press, 1998.

Hassan, Ihab., *The Literature of Silence: Henry Miller and Samuel Beckett*. Peter Smith: New York, 1967

Hutchings, William, "*Waiting for Godot* and the Principle of Uncertainty" in *Approaches to Teaching Beckett's Waiting for Godot* ed. June Schlueter and Enoch Brater. New York: The Modern Language Association of America, 1991

Kenner, Hugh, *A Reader's Guide to Samuel Beckett*. London: Thames and Hudson, 1973

Knowlson, James, *Damned to Fame: The Life of Samuel Beckett*. London: Bloomsbury, 1996

Knowlson, James (ed.), *The Theatrical Notebooks of Samuel Beckett, Volume 1: 'Waiting for Godot'*. London: Faber, 1992

Levy, Shimon, *Samuel Beckett's Self-Referential Drama: The Three I's.* New York: St Martin's Press, 1990

Lukács, Georg, 'The Ideology of Modernism'. In *Marxist Literary Theory* . Ed. by Eagleton & Milne. Oxford: Blackwell, 1996

Martin, Jean, "Creating Godot" in *Beckett in Dublin*. Dublin: The Lilliput Press, 1992

McDonald, Ronan, *Tragedy and Irish Literature: Synge, O'Casey, Beckett*. Basingstoke: Palgrave, 2002

McMillan, Dougald and Martha Fehsenfeld, *Beckett in the Theatre: The Author as Practical Playwright and Director: Volume 1*: From '*Waiting for Godot*' to '*Krapp's Last Tape*'. London: John Calder, 1988

Mercier, Vivian, *Beckett/Beckett*. New York: Oxford University Press, 1977

Pattie, David, *The Complete Critical Guide to Samuel Beckett*. London and New York: Routledge, 2000

Pountney, Rosemary and Nicholas Zurbrugg, *Waiting for Godot*. Longman: York Press, 1981

Pountney, Rosemary, *Theatre of Shadows: Samuel Beckett's Drama 1956-76*. Gerrards Cross: Colin Smythe, 1998

Reid, Alec, *All I Can Manage, More than I Could: An Approach to the Plays of Samuel Beckett*. Dublin: Dolmen Press, 1968

Ricks, Christopher, *Beckett's Dying Words*. Oxford: Oxford University Press,1993

Schlueter, June and Brater, Enoch (eds.), *Approaches to Teaching Beckett's Waiting for Godot*. New York: The Modern Language Association of America, 1991)

Schneider, Alan, *Entrances: An American Director's Journal*. New York: Viking, 1986

States, Bert O, *The Shape of Paradox: An Essay on Waiting for Godot*. Berkeley and Los Angeles: University of California Press, 1978

Webb, Eugene, *The Plays of Samuel Beckett*. Seattle: University of Washington Press, 1972

Worth, Katherine, *Samuel Beckett's Theatre: Life Journeys*. Oxford: Clarendon Press, 1999

First published in 2015 by
Connell Guides
Artist House
35 Little Russell Street
London WC1A 2HH

10 9 8 7 6 5 4 3 2 1

Copyright © The Connell Guides
All rights reserved. No part of this publication
may be reproduced, stored in a retrieval system or transmitted in any
form, or by any means (electronic, mechanical, or otherwise) without
the prior written permission of both the copyright owners
and the publisher.

Picture credits:
p.13 © Alastair Muir/REX_Shutterstock
p.21 © Alamy BGKPCP
p.35 © Donald Cooper/REX_Shutterstock

p. 28 Five facts about Beckett & *Waiting for Godot*
supplied by Connell Guides

A CIP catalogue record for this book is available from the British Library.
ISBN 978-1-907776-78-6

Design © Nathan Burton
Written by Sophie Ratcliffe
Edited by Jolyon Connell

Assistant Editors and typeset by
Paul Woodward & Holly Bruce

www.connellguides.com